Presented to:

Never Forget The Difference You've Made

Printed in Great Britain
by Amazon

31682802R00066